FOLLOW YOUR STUFF

Who Makes It, Where Does It Come From, How Does It Get to You?

Kevin Sylvester and **Michael Hlinka**

 annick press
toronto + berkeley

To Kit, Hap, Kathy, and Al — K.S.

Dedicated to Wyatt: The best thing
that ever happened to me! — M.H.

© 2019 Kevin Sylvester and Michael Hlinka (text)
© 2019 Kevin Sylvester (illustrations)
Second printing, August 2019

Edited by Linda Pruessen
Designed by Danielle Arbour

Annick Press Ltd.

We acknowledge the support of the Canada Council for the Arts and the Ontario Arts Council, and the participation of the Government of Canada/la participation du gouvernement du Canada for our publishing activities.

Cataloging in Publication

Sylvester, Kevin, author
        Follow your stuff : who makes it, where does it come
from, how does it get to you? / Kevin Sylvester, Michael Hlinka.

Issued in print and electronic formats.
ISBN 978-1-77321-254-8 (hardcover).--ISBN 978-1-77321-253-1
(softcover).--ISBN 978-1-77321-256-2 (HTML).--ISBN 978-1-77321-255-5
(PDF)

        1. Consumption (Economics)--Juvenile literature. 2. Consumer
goods--Juvenile literature. 3. Consumer behavior--Juvenile literature.
4. Economics--Juvenile literature. I. Hlinka, Michael, author II. Title.

HC79.C6S99 2019   j306.3   C2018-903733-4
                                                             C2018-903734-2

Published in the U.S.A. by Annick Press (U.S.) Ltd.
Distributed in Canada by University of Toronto Press.
Distributed in the U.S.A. by Publishers Group West.

Printed in China

annickpress.com
kevinsylvester.online
michaelhlinka.com

Also available as an e-book.
Please visit annickpress.com/ebooks for more details.

CONTENTS

Getting Ready to GO GLOBAL!

Who made the shirt you're wearing? Do you know? Can you say where it was made without looking at the tag?

The truth is, all of the things we use, consume, and buy are made by other people. Lots of them. Millions of them, in fact, from every part of the globe! People you will never meet. People who might not even know that their own good work helped you stay warm during the last bit of cold weather or helped you see better.

But wait, you say. I've made a cake . . . from scratch!

Not really. "From scratch" means you have access to the basic ingredients, but you are just assembling them. That cake is delicious, sure, but it's not really something you made all by yourself.

Someone else grew the wheat. Someone else harvested the sugarcane, and other people turned that into the sugar you used. Same thing for the flour, the milk, the icing, the food coloring, the chocolate, the candles, the . . . you get the idea.

Who are these people?
Where do they live?
How do they do their work?

Well, if this book had been written even 50 years ago, many of those people might have been your neighbors or lived pretty close to you. Today, thanks to cheaper transportation costs, advances in technology, and other issues we'll look at in the book, they probably live thousands of miles away.

Together, they form a chain of connections from, say, a cotton seed or a bit of rock to the shirt on your back, the phone in your hand, or THIS VERY BOOK!

And when you make a purchase, each one of them gets a tiny fraction of what you pay. Some get way smaller fractions than others—which raises a few questions about the fairness of this global economy.*

THIS VERY BOOK will attempt to explain who those people are, where they are (hint: everywhere!), what they do, how they get paid, and how you are involved in the global economy.

Okay, fasten your seat belts (made in Mexico) and strap on your safety goggles (made in Canada with raw materials from Indonesia), turn the page, and **GET READY TO GO GLOBAL!**

When we talk about a "global economy," we mean that raw materials and products come from all over the world and are sold all over the world. This "global" market has always been true for some products (such as tea, oil, and spices), but today it's true for almost everything.

Good Global QUESTIONS

Wait a minute: we're not quite ready to go global yet.

Before we get started, we have to deal with a huge issue.

"Is it worth it?"

You need to ask this question every time you're about to make a purchase—a purchase that will have an effect, remember, around the world. In fact, it's such an important question that it does double duty: you can (and should) ask it in two ways, neither of which is answered with a simple **yes or no.**

RELATIVE VALUE

$50

$50

**ONE:
Is it (whatever it is)
worth paying for?**

Most of us don't have endless supplies of money, so when we buy something, we have to determine if the expense is worth it. Is it worth parting with our hard-earned allowance to have this thing?

Another way to ask this question is, "What's worth more? A $50 video game or a $50 pair of jeans?"

Of course, it's a trick question. They both cost $50. But, you might be willing to pay $50 for one and not for the other. This is a really important concept known as "relative value." Here, "relative" means that different things are worth more (or less) to different people, even if they are priced the same.

The people who make goods and the people who sell them are constantly balancing what they can charge for an item versus what it costs them to make that item. If no one wants a video game, then it's not

worth $50. And this price target moves all the time. Want to pay $2,000 for a metal furrowing plow? No. But 100 years ago, you would have gladly shelled out the money because the plow was something you wanted and needed.

Manufacturers (the people and companies that make goods) try to cut or control costs while still making a profit. So they might shop for cheaper raw materials such as cotton or computer chips. Reducing costs lets them both lower prices and increase profits.

Another cost they can control is wages. Which leads us to . . .

People get paid to make the goods you buy. They are compensated for their skill and labor. In a perfect world, people doing the same job would be paid according to their skill and how hard they work. But actually, how much they get paid could depend more on where they live than how well they do their job.

A textile worker in Germany might get paid $15 an hour to make a shirt, while a person doing the same job in Guatemala might get $1. So, a shirt made in Guatemala might be cheaper for you to buy, but that's only because someone is getting paid a lot less to make it.

Not everyone agrees on whether that's a good thing or a bad thing. In fact, there are no simple answers when it comes to questions about "fair wages."

In Germany, $15 an hour is about the minimum wage and just slightly below the average hourly wage for all workers.

In Guatemala, $1 an hour is well above the average wage. That tells us a lot about the different poverty levels in the two countries, and it also shows why a textile company might move a factory to Guatemala rather than pay higher wages in Germany.

Should they pay their workers more? Good question. And that's just scratching the surface of the ways in which wages affect the global economy.

$1

Throughout the book, you will see big question marks like the one above. They're telling you that it's time to start thinking more deeply about a particular issue. Maybe it's the wage of the miners who dug the ore that was used to make your cell phone. Or perhaps it's safety concerns about the product itself. A lot of fuel is burned to move things around the globe, so that environmental impact is also something to consider.

We're not going to answer the questions. But you need to ask them every time you buy something.

You are a huge part of the global economy, and every dollar you spend is part of a system that touches dozens of lives directly, and millions indirectly.

Okay, now we're ready to go.

$15

T-SHIRT?
More Like A-to-Z-shirt!

There are dozens of people (at least) who helped turn a living plant into the cotton T-shirt on your back.

That's a cool-looking tee you just picked up at the Fits U 2 a T shop at your local mall. It's even got the logo for your favorite band, the Globals. Let's say you paid $25 for it (plus $2.50 in tax* that goes to the government). Who got what?

Let's start at the beginning.

* Taxes vary depending on where you live or shop. To keep it simple, when we talk about tax in the book, we've rounded it to an even 10 percent.

One more thing to clear up before we move on. Throughout the book, we'll discuss "profit." But there are two kinds.

GROSS profit is what's left over after subtracting the direct costs of making a product from the selling price. So, for example, if it costs a company $10 to make a pair of pants and they sell those pants for $40, they've made a gross profit of $30.

But there are other costs that businesses have to consider— things such as rent, insurance, electricity, and so on. Once those costs are taken into account, there's less than $30 left. This is the NET profit. And if the total cost to produce and sell the product is more than the selling price of the product, that's a LOSS.

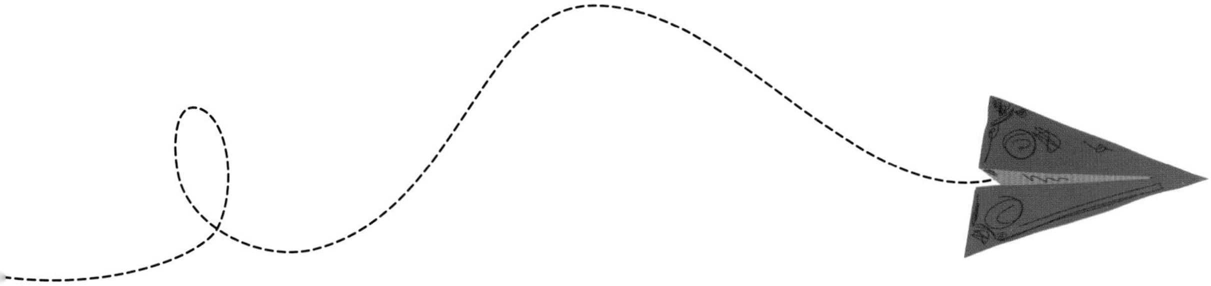

$25

TOTAL COST

A (COT)TON OF FUN

It all starts with a seed. Cotton is grown all over the world, but the cotton in your shirt came from a farm in China.

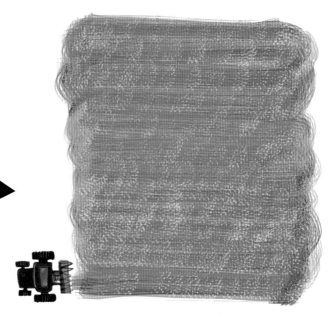

The farmer uses a machine to sow thousands of seeds in a field, which is divided into acres—squares about 64 meters by 64 meters (209 feet by 209 feet). Then she pays for fertilizer, water, and workers to make sure the plants yield a good harvest.

She might use a machine to harvest the cotton, or she might use workers. They get paid about $15 per acre—from seed to harvest. That's not a lot for months of labor.

There is often a conflict between profit and human rights. A few countries use incredibly cheap labor, or even forced labor, to harvest crops. That makes your T-shirt much cheaper for you to buy, but is it worth it?

COSTS per acre:

Seeds:	$100.00
Fertilizer/pesticide:	$100.00
Water:	$4.00
Machinery costs:	$50.00
Labor/wages:	$15.00
Business costs (repairs, fuel, insurance):	$150.00
TOTAL:	**$419.00**

Each acre yields the farmer about 500 pounds (226.80 kilograms) of cotton. Cotton prices vary, but let's say the average is $1 per pound (0.45 kilogram). That means the farmer has made $500 from her cotton per acre, but she spent $419 to get that.

PROFIT*:

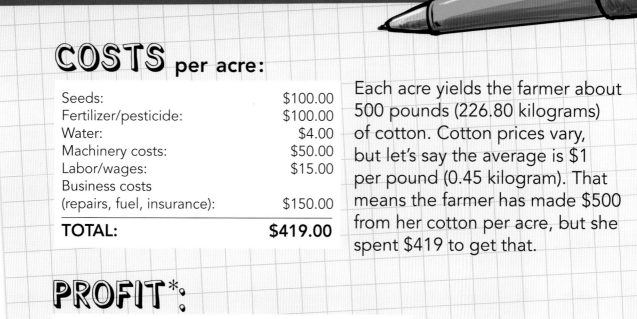

500 pounds of cotton at $1/pound **=** **$500** **SUBTOTAL** **–** **$419** **COSTS** **=** **$81** **TOTAL**

(although the farmer invests much of this back into the farm for upgrades to buildings, machinery, and so on)

*The net profit might be higher or lower, depending on the day. Commodities (like cotton, beef, and oil or gas) are subject to price changes based on "supply and demand." If a storm wipes out a huge part of the cotton crop, the supply is low (scarcity) and prices go up. But if it's a perfect year and there is too much cotton (a glut), prices can drop a lot.

1 pound (0.45 kilogram). **=** **16** ounces (453.6 grams).

= **6** ounces (170 grams).

There are 16 ounces (453.6 grams) in a pound, and a T-shirt contains about 6 ounces (170 grams) of cotton. That means the cotton only makes up about $0.38* of the cost of your shirt.

★$1 x 6/16 ounces of cotton = **$0.38**

At the end of this stage, we've got an extremely large pile of cotton balls, picked and ready to be sent to a factory that will turn them into woven fabric.

CREATING CLOTH

The raw cotton is sent to a textile manufacturer. These can be found all over the world, but the fabric for this shirt was made in Guatemala.

Many textile workers are known as "unskilled laborers." This means that their work can be done by almost anyone, with a little bit of training. This leads some companies to offer poor working conditions, including long hours for low wages. If employees don't like it, there's not much they can do. Would you pay more if you knew it would raise wages for those workers?

The cotton balls are fed into a series of machines. They are spun into thin strands and then woven into sheets. The workers get paid about $325 a month.*

A T-shirt is made from about 1 meter (3.28 feet) of fabric, and it takes about 10 minutes, from start to finish, to make that in the factory.

*In Sri Lanka, textile workers make about $60 a month; in Turkey, they might get $850 a month. Workers in North America might get $2,600.

COSTS per T-shirt:

Wages:	$0.10
Factory/machinery:	$0.25
Chemicals* for treating fabric:	$0.20
Dyes for making it green:	$0.30
Markup:	$0.20
TOTAL:	**$1.05**

* Chemicals are used throughout this process. They're needed to clean the fibers as they are spun and woven. Cotton is often bleached, for example, to make sure it is evenly white. And since the Globals love yellow, the fabric will be dyed before it's sent to the factory that assembles the shirt.

The textile factory buys the chemicals and dyes from factories in China and the United States.

The total cost of the shirt, in materials and wages, is now about $1.43

$0.38 + $1.05 = $1.43

COTTON   CLOTH   COST

Rolls of cloth are now ready to be shipped to a factory that will cut, sew, and assemble the shirts.

STITCHING IT TOGETHER

The cotton—now in fabric form— has arrived at an assembly plant. Check the tag on your shirt. It says India? That means your shirt was put together at a factory there.

The pressure to make clothes quickly and cheaply can lead factories to become "sweatshops." People are crammed into decaying buildings, working long hours on overheating machines, with few or no breaks and for little or no money. In 2012, a deadly fire at a factory in Bangladesh showed how horrible, and dangerous, those conditions can be. More than 100 people died after the building caught fire. Do you know the working conditions where your shirt was made? How can you find out?

A worker known as a "cutter" literally cuts the cotton sheets according to the pattern* the company gives her. The cutter makes about $105 a month and cuts hundreds of pieces in that time.

Once the fabric is cut, it's sewn together by a seamstress. She might sit at a sewing machine at the factory, or take pieces home to assemble the shirts and then bring them back to the factory for shipping. Either way, she makes about $125 a month and will assemble hundreds of shirts.

Both workers make just a few cents for every shirt they measure, cut, and sew.

*That pattern was developed by a designer in Canada. He was paid a one-time fee, so that doesn't add much to the cost of the shirt. But without his design, it wouldn't fit properly.

COSTS per T-shirt:

Wages:	$0.65
Machinery:	$2.00
Factory (power, fuel, etc.):	$1.00
Rent/insurance:	$1.00
Thread*:	$0.02
Agent:	$0.20
Storage:	$0.10
Markup:	$0.90
TOTAL:	**$5.87**

The seamstress uses nylon thread to sew the T-shirt's arms and body together. The thread comes from a lab in Mexico. It costs about $0.02 per shirt and is a by-product of the petroleum industry. A by-product is what's left over after making fuel from crude oil.

The total cost of the assembled shirt, in materials and wages, is now about $7.30.

$0.38 + **$1.05** + **$5.87** = **$7.30**

COTTON   CLOTH   STITCHING   COST

But it still needs that awesome logo.

THE GLOBALS Get Their Cut

> The logo is stamped onto the fabric using a process known as silk-screening.

Some people think it's okay to use images without paying the artist. Knockoffs, or fakes, are usually much cheaper than the real thing and are available online or on street-corner markets the world over. Maybe the super-famous Globals won't feel the hit so much, but the designer will. Each illegal sale hurts his ability to make a living. Should you pay extra for an official shirt?

Sometimes the logo might be added at the same factory in India. But this time, it's done by yet another factory in Mexico.

A printer operates the machine that stamps the logo onto each shirt. He gets paid about $150 a month and prints a Globals' logo on a shirt about every minute. This includes placing the shirt on a press, angling it properly, and then letting it dry.

At least four other people then fold the dried shirts, seal them in plastic, and box them for shipping to the store.

COSTS per T-shirt:

Wages:	$0.50
Factory costs (power, fuel, etc.):	$0.20
Ink:	$0.10
Royalties* (to the band):	$1.00
Markup:	$0.90
TOTAL:	**$2.70**

Royalties are money paid to artists for the right to use their name, artwork, logo, etc. The T-shirt manufacturer knows they can charge more for an official Globals shirt than they can for a normal yellow shirt. So they agree to pay a bit of the price of every shirt to the band.

The band didn't design the logo. They hired a designer who lives in Los Angeles to design one. And they give him a 10 percent royalty on every sale, or $0.10.

The total cost of the shirt is now $10.

$0.38 + $1.05 + $5.87 + $2.70 = $10.00

COTTON   CLOTH   STITCHING   LOGO   COST

The shirt is *finally* packaged and sent to the store. And the journey isn't over yet!

ON THE ROAD

Before you put down your hard-earned cash, there's a huge part of the equation that we need to cover. Transportation.

Transportation factors in to every stage of the T-shirt process. And each time your shirt (in whatever form) takes to the road, a fraction more is added to the cost of the final product.

And, of course, there are many people involved in moving the materials around.

The raw cotton is delivered from the farm to a shipping container* that takes the cotton to Guatemala. Dockworkers unload the cargo and put it on a truck to the factory.

That process repeats itself from the textile factory in

Guatemala to the garment factory in India, and then to the silk-screen plant in Mexico. And again from Mexico to the T-shirt company's warehouse, and then from there to the store in your hometown. There might even be a train or plane involved.

Gigantic cargo ships stacked with shipping containers have revolutionized global transport. Goods, like T-shirts, can be transported by the millions for just pennies an item. The cost can go up or down depending on global prices for fuel, but because these ships are so huge, the additional costs get spread over many items.

Between shipping, trucking, and wages, the total transportation costs are about $1.61 per shirt—which brings the total cost of your shirt, so far, to $11.61.

$0.38 + $1.05 + $5.87 + $2.70 + $1.61 =

COTTON   CLOTH   STITCHING   LOGO   TRANSPORTATION

$11.61

COST

But wait. You paid $25, so where does the other $13.39 go? Finally, we get to you and the shop.

CLOSING the Deal

You decide to get a new T-shirt, so you head to the mall to visit your favorite place— the Fits U 2 a T shop.

The store paid the T-shirt manufacturer $15 to buy the shirt.

But didn't it cost $11.61 to make? Yup. But that extra $3.39 is the "markup" the manufacturer adds to make sure they can cover their costs and make a profit. If the store is owned by the manufacturer (like, say, a big clothing store), that cost is just added to the price. But Fits U 2 a T is a small business, so they buy the shirt from the manufacturer.

Now the storeowner has to decide how much she needs to charge above that to cover her costs.

COSTS per T-shirt:

Wages:	$1.00
Rent:	$1.00
Insurance:	$0.05
Electricity:	$0.50
Heat:	$0.50
Racks and displays:	$0.24
Advertising:	$0.10
TOTAL:	**$3.39**

The owner decides the markup she needs is $10. So the total cost of the shirt is $25.

$0.38 + $1.05 + $5.87 + $2.70 + $1.61 + $3.39 + $10.00 = $25

COTTON   CLOTH   STITCHING   LOGO   TRANSPORTATION   MANU-FACTURER MARKUP   RETAIL MARKUP   COST

What costs?

Well, there are many. Electricity, rent, insurance, taxes, and more.

The salesperson gets about $12 an hour.* You took around five minutes to make your choice, so she made about $1 of that selling you the shirt and ringing it into the system.

*Sometimes a salesperson gets a portion of each sale added to their salary; that's called a "commission." So the more they sell, the more they make. Say they make a 10 percent commission and sell $100 worth of clothes. That means they'd make $10 on the total sales.

That leaves a profit of $6.65 for the store. The owner takes her pay out of that, but she also uses some of the money to buy more shirts and to cover losses on things that don't sell.

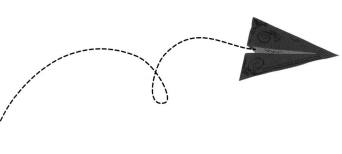

PAUSE for the People

One more break before we wrap things up.

Right at the beginning of this book, we said that there are people all over the world making either the thing you use or the various parts of it. We called it a "chain" of people.

This is a really important point, and these are real people, so we want to pause to show just how HUGE this chain actually is.

So, let's look at your T-shirt from the perspectives of the people involved.

There's the farmer who planted the cottonseed.

But that farmer relies on the people who make the fertilizer.

The people who make the fertilizer rely on the chemists who work out the formula. Or, if it's organic fertilizer, the dairy farmer whose cows produce the manure. And that farmer relies on the people who make feed, and the veterinarians who make sure the animals are healthy. And they all rely on the medicine manufacturers who make sure that happens.

And that's just to get one seed planted and growing. But each stage before and after connects to other people.

There are machines. They start off as minerals in the ground. So, you have miners and engineers and geologists doing their jobs. And how about the people who make the food that keeps all of the other people working?

There are computers. They also rely on miners—but programmers and chip manufacturers, too.

The bottom line is that the deeper you look, the more you realize that almost EVERYONE who does a job is somehow related to that shirt.

Here's a fun game. Name a job. Any kind of job. Can you draw a connection from that job to your T-shirt?

IN CONCLUSION and In Your Shirt

Your simple shirt doesn't seem so simple anymore, does it? And we haven't even mentioned the people who made the computer the salesperson uses to enter the sale. Or the people at the bank who process the transaction. Or the people who designed the chip in your plastic credit card (also made with a petroleum by-product), or . . . well, you get the picture.

So, just to recap how we got from seed to store:

COSTS per T-shirt:

Farmers in China:	$0.38
Textile workers in Guatemala:	$1.05
Garment makers in India and scientists around the world:	$5.87
Silk-screeners in Mexico, and the Globals:	$2.70
All those truck drivers, dockworkers, pilots, and train engineers:	$1.61
Markup for the manufacturing company:	$3.39
Shopkeeper and sales staff in your hometown:	$10.00
TOTAL:	**$25.00**

$0.38 + $1.05 + $5.87 + $2.70 + $1.61 + $3.39 + $10.00 = **$25**

COTTON + CLOTH + STITCHING + LOGO + TRANSPORTATION + MANU-FACTURER MARKUP + RETAIL MARKUP = TOTAL COST

? A lot of carbon was used to make your shirt. Think about the gas burned in farm equipment or each time a truck, boat, or airplane moved the product or the raw materials from place to place. Does it make more sense to try to buy something made closer to home? Maybe, but it will actually cost more, thanks to the higher wages in North America, and it might actually have a higher carbon footprint. When large amounts of raw materials are shipped together, the trucks, for example, might burn a lot of fuel, but the portion per shirt is actually very small.

And just look at how far the bits of that T-shirt traveled to make it to your hometown. **That's a total of 47,918.01 kilometers (29,774.87 miles).**

Is the story of your T-shirt typical? In some ways, yes. Wages and transportation, for example, are part of every product's story. But other products take their own unique path through the global economy . . .

PUFFERS and MEDS

Almost everyone takes medication when they're sick or when they need some help to regulate their bodies or minds.

So you've got asthma,* and it turns out your friend's new T-shirt is covered in his pet cat's hair. Yikes! Your eyes begin to water and your lungs fill up. Grab that puffer!

Asthma sufferers often use inhalers—or "puffers." The medicine opens up the airways and relaxes the muscles in the lungs and chest, helping people take in more oxygen. Ah, relief!

The price of that puffer depends on where you live. In Canada, for example, the cost might be around $40 per puffer. In the United States, it might be closer to $200. **Why?**

* "Asthma" comes from the Greek word for "breathe hard." It's a condition that's described in many early stories. Some suggested treatments included eating chicken soup and drinking owl's blood.

Well, lots of reasons (and we'll explore some of them in more detail as we chart the puffer and its parts around the globe), but two big ones:

Government policy. Some governments have health systems that cover some of the costs, so the price you pay at the pharmacy isn't the full price. Governments can also set price limits on drugs, preventing companies from overcharging.

Insurance coverage. Your family might have private health insurance that covers part or all of the price of the drug. So, the pharmacy charges you the full price—say, $200—but you get reimbursed all or part of that. (Of course, if you don't have insurance or can't afford it, you have to pay the full price yourself.)

For the purpose of our discussion, we'll look at a $60 puffer.

Take a deep breath, and let's go.

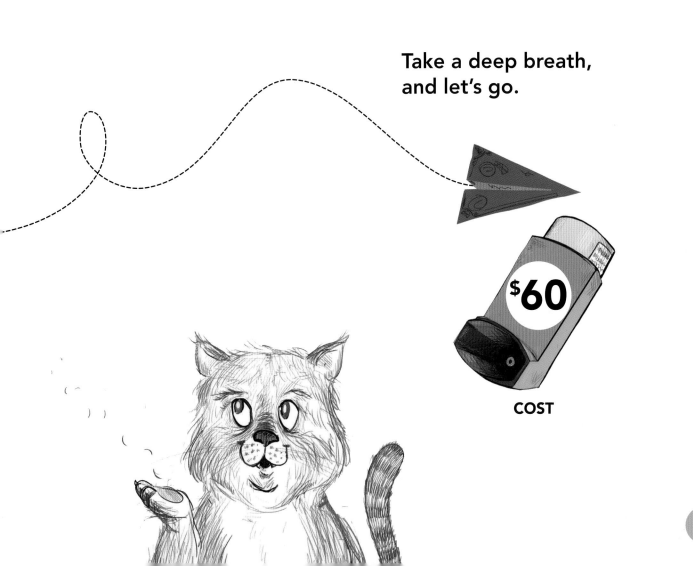

COST

TAKE A DEEP BREATH

People have suffered from breathing problems since . . . well, since the beginning of people.

Early healers have connected the breathing in of medicines to helping people recover, while the Ancient Egyptians suggested inhaling the smoke from burning medicinal herbs.

About 250 years ago, English doctor John Mudge made the first "puffer"—a tin cup with a hole poked in the lid. Patients filled the cup with hot water and whatever drug the doctor prescribed (often opium, a serious narcotic). They'd heat it and breathe in the steam through a small tube.

In the late 1800s, Dr. Allen DeVilbiss developed a device called an "atomizer." A squeezable bulb forced air over a container of liquid medicine, combining the two into a mist. His company later manufactured these for perfumes.

These treatments were only available to those who could afford private doctors and expensive drugs.

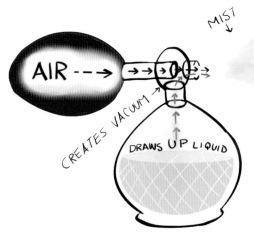

American doctor George Maison designed the modern inhaler/puffer in the 1950s. It used high pressure to pack a lot of medicine inside. This puffer was portable and cheaper than the previous century's bulky inhalers, and patients could take a puff when they felt an asthma attack coming on. His daughter had asthma.

Inventors, doctors, and drug companies have worked to streamline the puffer ever since. Along the way, they've changed the drugs inside as well as the way the puffer works.

One of the most common medicines used is salbutamol.*

Salbutamol was created in the late 1960s by English chemists and is on the World Health Organization's list of "essential medicines"—a kind of shopping list for countries that want to set up a health system.

Our puffer manufacturer is Global Goods Pharmaceuticals (GGP).

Let's see how they make a puffer in our modern world.

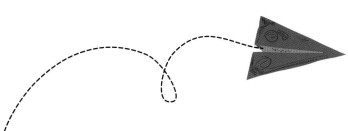

Getting the
RAW MATERIALS

To make salbutamol, GGP needs raw materials to make the chemicals.

One of these is sulfuric acid—not in a dose high enough to burn, but enough to relax the lung muscles.

To make sulfuric acid, you need sulfur. It is available as a petroleum by-product. But the traditional method is mining it from the ground. Common sources are Indonesia, Chile, and Japan.

Sodium chloride is another substance in salbutamol. It's basically salt, and salt comes from—you guessed it—mining. It's slightly cheaper to buy than sulfuric acid.

Sulfur is a natural by-product of volcanic eruptions, and one of the biggest mines in the world is inside an active volcano in Indonesia named Ijen. Workers actually break off chunks by hand and carry it out in baskets. The miners earn an average of about $8 a day. They carry the raw sulfur 3 kilometers (1.86 miles) to a nearby town. Does that seem like a fair wage for that work?

GGP buys sulfur for $125 a ton and sends it to a processing plant in Russia. The sulfur is burned, cooled, heated, and cooled again in a series of tanks. Water is added to the gas at the end, creating the acid—1 ton of sulfur makes 3 tons of acid.

Chemists control and monitor the process. Other technicians control the quality of the water, maintain the machinery, and store the final product in specialized tanks.

The company sells the sulfuric acid for $200 a ton, but only a fraction will be used to make salbutamol—there's less than 1/100 of a milligram inside each puffer, and there are 1 billion milligrams in 1 ton. Thanks to the teeny, tiny amount used, the combined minerals and chemicals have added just a few cents (about $0.04) to the total cost of your puffer.

But a lot of people have helped get the acid to the next stage—GGP laboratories.

Making the MEDICINE

Chemists at the GGP labs combine raw materials into compounds that we call medicines.

The raw materials are shipped in special container trucks to GGP's manufacturing plant in New Jersey. It's a giant lab where everything inside is as clean and sterile as possible.

The sulfuric acid and sodium chloride are loaded into special tanks, called "reactors," that will cause the chemical reactions that turn the raw compounds into the medicine you take. A lot of water and energy are used in the process.

A team of chemists monitors the assembly of the medicine according to a pre-set formula. They'll test each batch of finished medicine along the way for impurities.

The suits the workers wear resemble astronaut outfits. They keep the workers safe from some pretty serious materials and keep outside stuff, like hair, from getting into the meds. These suits are made by a company that specializes in safety equipment. They are made from synthetic fabrics such as plastics, latex, and rubber.

COSTS

per puffer:

Wages:	$1.00
Machinery:	$1.50
Water:	$0.005
Electricity:	$0.01
Plastics:	$0.07
TOTAL:	**$2.59**

The next stage is getting the pressurized gas inside the puffer canisters. This process is heavily automated* but watched over by a trained technician, or quality control officer.

The metal canisters are made by GGP at a factory in Turkey. They contain a valve that controls the dosage of medicine released with each push.

Automation is a huge part of the modern economy. Many jobs that used to be done by people are now done by robots and machines. Some of these jobs (like dealing with chemicals) are incredibly dangerous. Some (like putting parts of a car together) are just cheaper if done by a robot rather than a person.

The plant packages thousands of puffers a day. There are high costs for everything from wages to transportation. But with so many drugs being made, these costs are spread over millions of medications.

At this point, the total cost for the actual puffer and what's inside is around $2.63.

$0.04 **+** $2.59 **=** $2.63

CHEMICALS   MANUFACTURING

COST

So, where do the other costs come from? Well, the biggest one comes before the drug is actually made . . . long before.

Testing and TESTING and...

Laboratories don't just manufacture medications; they also research new treatment methods. And that isn't easy. Or cheap...

Research and testing is the main reason drug companies give for the high costs of medications. There might only be a few cents' worth of chemicals in a puffer, but the companies also recoup the money and time they spent developing that formula and making sure it was safe and effective.

A study found that drug companies spend nearly $3 billion developing just one drug that eventually makes it to market. Right now, there are thousands of drugs being developed and tested around the world. In the United States, the Food and Drug Administration only approves about 40 to 50 a year.

Let's say a new illness shows up that is caused by a particularly mean germ—X23D.

GGP scientists examine the makeup of X23D. Using computers and years of education and experience, they'll predict what meds might work to neutralize or eliminate it. They'll mix up different chemical compounds to test and hope that one works.

GGP starts testing in "preclinical" trials. These take place only in the lab, often in test tubes. The trials tell the scientists a lot. Some of the mixtures might work on X23D, for example, but be too toxic for humans to consume. Others might not work at all or work only a little bit.

So the scientists tweak and test and retest until they find a mix of molecules that takes out X23D and looks like it will also be safe for humans.

$0.04 + $2.59 + ? = $2.63+

CHEMICALS   MANUFACTURING   TESTING   COST

But we're still a looooooooooong way from the drug making it to market.

...TESTING and...TESTING and...

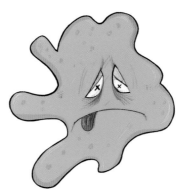

> A drug might work inside a lab, but if it doesn't work inside you, what's the point?

Once GGP has a drug they think could work, they ask the government for approval to run clinical trials. These might start with tests on animals, to see if the drug does what GGP thinks it will do—and if it's safe.

Human trials are next. These start small (usually with a group of volunteers) and then grow. If the new drug seems to eliminate X23D safely and effectively, it's approved. Once that happens, doctors can start prescribing it, and GGP will start manufacturing it.

But even then, it might take years before GGP knows just how effective the new drug is. Does it work over a long period of time? Does it work on only a small number of people with X23D? Or does it work on almost all? Are there long-term side effects that show up years after taking the drug?

Researchers, clinicians, nurses, and doctors at GGP, in the government, and from universities will study these things for years. All of that costs money.

Drugs are often tested on animals, such as mice or rats, before being cleared for trials on humans. The animals might be deliberately infected with X23D to see how the drug works. There's a big debate over whether that's fair. There's also debate over whether animal reactions are an accurate predictor of how a drug will work on humans. Is it okay to test drugs on animals as a way to see if they will help humans?

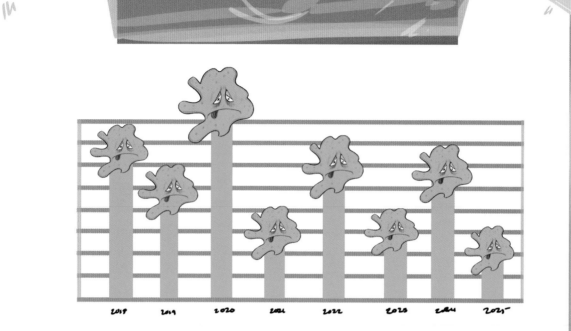

Once GGP develops a new drug, they will patent it. This means they own that specific formula and no one else can make it without paying them.* This also allows them to recoup the costs of developing the drug, since they can set whatever selling price they want.

And medicine is big business.

Patents run out after 10 years or so. At that point, the formula becomes public, and other companies can make "generic" drugs. These almost always sell for less than the original.

BIG BUSINE$$

Drug companies provide the medicines that people need. But they also want to make a profit from the sales of their drugs.

And there's the (in)famous case of Martin Shkreli. His company, Turing Pharmaceuticals, bought the rights to the drug Daraprim and then raised the price—a lot. Before his company bought Daraprim, the price was $18 a pill. After? $750. Shkreli argued that his company simply needed to make more money. How would you balance profit and selling medicines for sick people?

GGP is a private company, with shareholders and thousands of employees. Shareholders are people who pay the company money to to help run the business; in return, they get a "share" of any profits. (They also risk losing money if the company loses money.) Those people need (and want) to be paid. The company also wants to apply profits from successful drugs toward research on other drugs, such as cancer treatments.

So GGP estimates the cost of getting a puffer to market as something like $2.63 for the puffer itself and an additional $35 to $42 to make back the money the company put into research, plus make a profit for shareholders. The cost of the testing stage for the puffer was calculated at $37.37, bringing the total now to $40.

Ever heard the term "Big Pharma"? It's not a compliment. Although governments regulate the industry, drug companies spend millions to "lobby," or influence, politicians to support laws that let companies do things like set their own prices.

There are other issues, too—cases where drug companies push for government approval before all the safety tests have been done. And some target doctors directly, offering them incentives to recommend their drug over another company's drug—whether it works better or not.

Big Pharma is a huge topic, though, and this is only meant as an introduction.

$0.04 + $2.59 + $37.37 = $40

CHEMICALS   MANUFACTURING   TESTING

COST

Back to our $60 puffer.

We've had hundreds of people doing their jobs— in mines, labs, and doctors' offices—to make the puffer and the medicine inside available to those who need it. That all adds up to about $40. So why do you pay $60 or more?

Setting the PRICE YOU PAY

The final stage of our journey takes us to your local pharmacy.

The pharmacist buys the puffer from GGP for $48 (giving the manufacturer an $8 markup). Then she adds another $10 markup and a $2 dispensing fee, meaning $20 gets added to the cost of the puffer.

Sometimes the last two items are combined, but the idea is that the markup covers normal store costs (calculated at $3.35 per puffer), and the fee covers costs directly related to the drug.

The pharmacist has undergone years of training to do her job. She doesn't just sell premixed drugs like your puffer. She also mixes drugs that have best-before dates, such as antibiotics.

She spent four years at college getting a doctorate (after spending at least three years getting an undergraduate degree). Students pay anywhere from $12,000 to $100,000 in tuition* during that time. So that's a debt she has to cover through her income. Still, it can be a lucrative business, with pharmacy owners earning upward of $200,000 a year.

Tuition varies widely depending on the school and where you live. If you go to school close to home, you might pay a local-student rate of $4,000 a year. If you go to a school in a different country, state, or province, you might pay $25,000 a year.

COSTS per puffer:

Wages:	$1.00
Rent:	$1.00
Insurance:	$0.05
Electricity:	$0.50
Heat:	$0.50
Racks and displays:	$0.20
Advertising:	$0.10
TOTAL:	**$3.35**

Not all drugs are prescription drugs, of course. But the process for development, pricing, and sales is similar whether you're looking to treat a headache or a disease or condition.

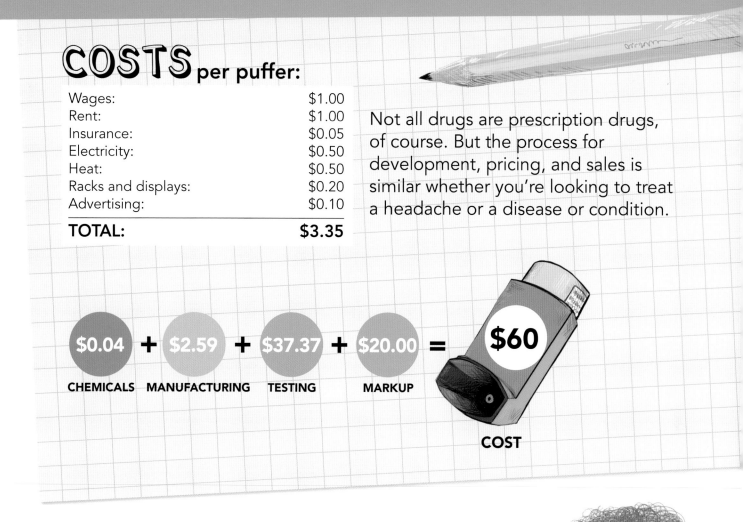

$0.04 + **$2.59** + **$37.37** + **$20.00** = **$60**

CHEMICALS   MANUFACTURING   TESTING   MARKUP   COST

? Another charge against drug companies is that they will overhype, or possibly even invent, health problems in order to sell meds to treat them. You are in charge of what you use, so make sure you know why your doctor wants you to take something. How do you make sure you have a condition that needs medication?

IN CONCLUSION and In Your Lungs

That puffer contains years of history and research along with its medications. And it has taken an incredible number of people with specific skills to get all of that inside.

So, just to recap how we got from minerals to your backpack:

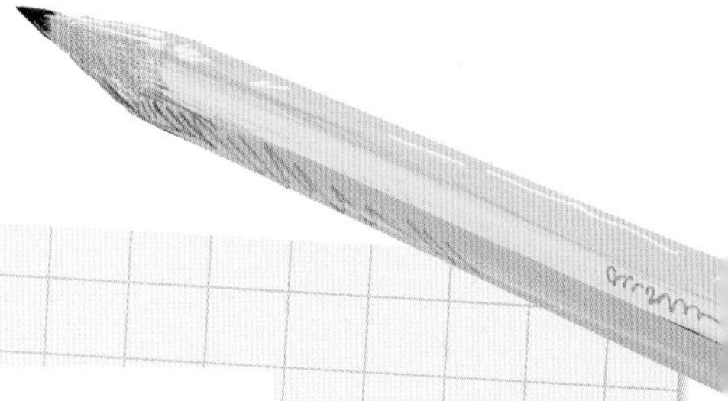

COSTS per puffer:

Mining raw resources:	$0.02
Processing chemicals:	$0.02
Making medicine from those chemicals:	$2.59
Research and testing:	$37.27
Markup for GGP:	$8.00
Local pharmacist:	$12.00
TOTAL:	**$60.00**

$0.04 + $2.59 + $37.37 + $8.00 + $12.00 = $60

CHEMICALS   MANUFACTURING   TESTING   MANUFACTURER MARKUP   PHARMACY MARKUP

TOTAL COST

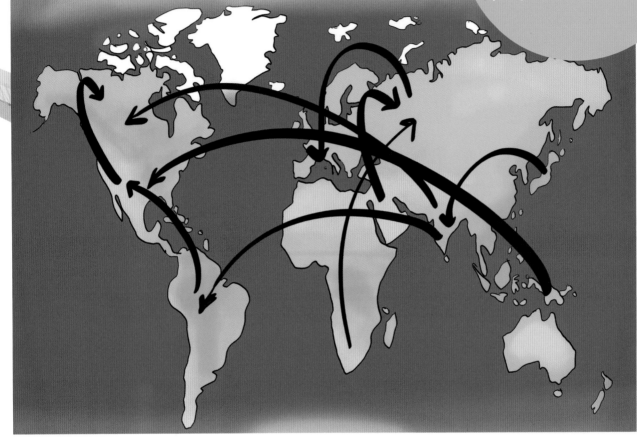

And just look at how far we've traveled to assemble that puffer. **That's a total of 34,319.58 kilometers (21,325.20 miles).**

See, this book is full of amazing facts and information! Next, let's look at how it was made!

This Very BOOK

Here's how *Follow Your Stuff* happened . . .

A few years ago, we wrote a book called *Follow Your Money*. It looked at who gets paid, and how much, when you buy stuff. After we were done, our publisher had a question. We'd talked about what people got paid, but we didn't go too deeply into how things were made or who made them. What about a book that looked at that?*

* This idea was sparked by a famous essay titled "I, Pencil" by economist Leonard E. Read. Read imagines a pencil telling its life story and talking about all the people who need to do their jobs—from mining to forestry and beyond—to make something that appears so simple.

We sat down over coffee (made by a local barista) and wrote down some ideas (in a notebook made in India). Kevin is a writer and illustrator of more than 20 books. Michael is an economist, teacher, and broadcaster. We combined our different backgrounds and skills to hammer out a proposal.

We suggested a list of products that would take you, the reader, around the world and into all the ways humans make stuff. Our publisher looked at it and said, "Okay, let's do this book."

This was in early 2017.

Follow Your Stuff is published by a small independent press called Annick. The bigger publishing houses might have bigger teams of editors, designers, and marketing experts, but every published book is made with teamwork. Not to mention editorial assistants, legal teams, electronic media people . . . and more. And those workers are all over the globe.

KEVIN ↓   MICHAEL ↓

Sign on the DOTTED LINE!

> Before we started researching, writing, and illustrating, we signed a contract with the publisher.

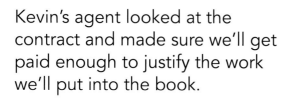

Kevin's agent looked at the contract and made sure we'll get paid enough to justify the work we'll put into the book.

Writers don't get an hourly wage (with rare exceptions). They have to deliver a manuscript by a certain date. And that can take hundreds of hours or just a few. It depends on each project, and you can't always predict before starting the work.

Annick knows we'll spend a lot of time preparing the book, so they agreed to pay us some money in advance. The total was $10,000.*

* Kevin got $3,500 on signing and $3,500 on the approval of the manuscript.

Michael got $1,500 on signing and $1,500 on the approval of the manuscript.

This is known as an "advance on royalties." Once the book is for sale, the authors will get a percentage of each transaction (more on that later). But they won't get paid until the money earned from that percentage matches the advance. Celebrities sometimes get HUGE advances—millions of dollars—for books their publishers think will sell millions of copies.

annick press

Excellence & Innovation
in Children's Literature

Ten percent of Kevin's advance goes to the agency that negotiated the contract. The agency's lawyers, agents, and other staff drum up other business, so this fee covers their salaries, as well as costs such as photocopying, mail, phones, and so on.

So, a lot of money has already been paid for a book that isn't even close to being written.

Time to get to work!

Get to WORK!

Annick's managing editor takes over the job of talking to Kevin and Michael about how things are going.

Kevin starts by looking at lots of different sources for how a T-shirt is made. (Many of these are included in "References and Further Reading" at the back of the book.)

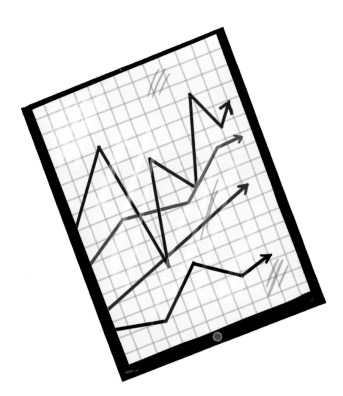

Michael looks at commodity indexes, stock markets, and company websites to determine how much a company pays for, say, baled cotton. And then he follows the chain to figure out how much cotton is in each shirt. Math, basically, and information-searching.

NO PROBLEM!

It's hard to put a value on how much everyone got paid, but let's say the total cost of the book, to date, is about $1,500. Add that to the first half of Kevin's and Michael's advances, and the total costs so far add up to $6,500.

That cost will be spread out over the individual books once they are published. So let's hold off on figuring out how much of that contributes to the price you pay for one book.

Michael and Kevin go back and forth for weeks, making sure the numbers match and the text makes sense. They meet for coffee a few times (thank you, coffee* growers in Kenya!), and after a few months, they have a rough outline and a sample chapter on T-shirts.

The publisher and managing editor go over it. "Close," they say, "but do some more work."

So Kevin and Michael go back to work.

The important thing at this stage is that Kevin and Michael and the folks at Annick have been putting in a lot of hours.

* Fair-trade organizations look at how much money coffee workers are paid, their working conditions, and the quality of the coffee. They can certify the coffee as "fair trade," which means (among other things) that the workers get paid a fair wage. But this coffee is almost always more expensive. Should a coffee drinker pay an extra $1 or $2 for a cup of fair-trade coffee?

REWRITING and REWRITING and REWRITING and...

Writing a book is a lot like doing a homework assignment in school. The first draft is never perfect, so you have to edit.

Kevin, Michael, and the team at Annick go back and forth writing and re-writing and researching and re-researching for months.

Once the text seems to fit, the manuscript is sent to a copy editor/fact-checker. That person looks for spelling eroors, math misteakkes, and other thinnnngs that need to be fixed. Kevin and Michael incorporate those changes into the manuscript.

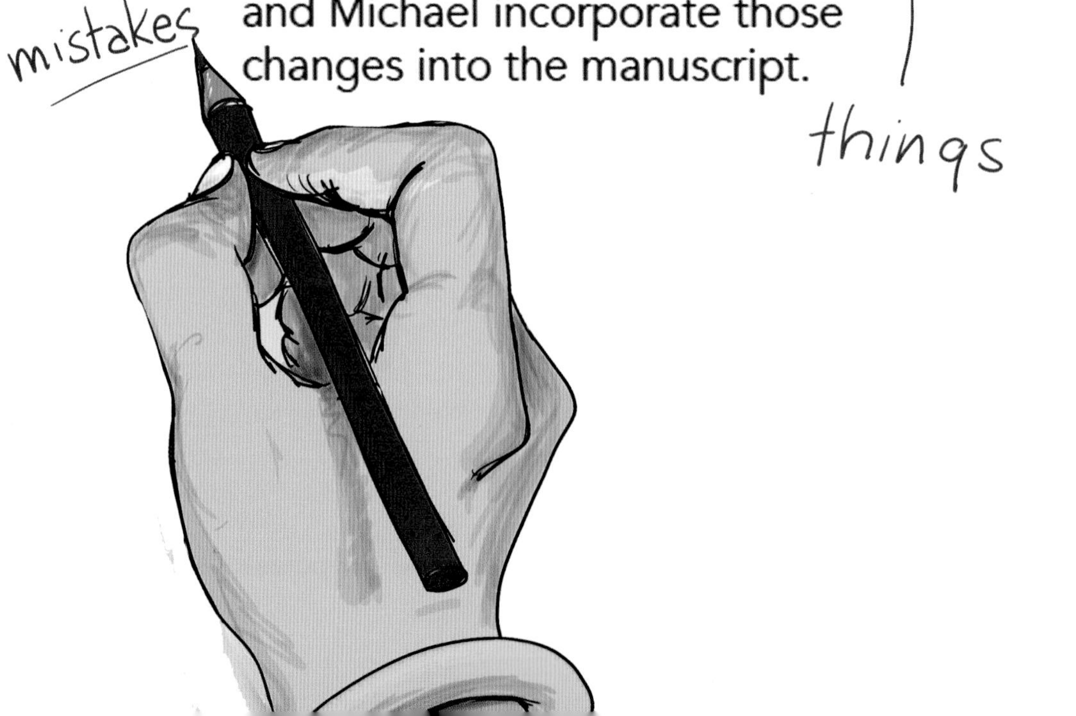

errors

mistakes

things

Next, it's time to do the images and design. Annick's art director and Kevin work out the final images (infographics, charts, and so on) that will accompany the text. She also designs the layout and chooses the various typefaces—or fonts—that are used. When she and Kevin are done, the book will be proofread and indexed before it is ready for printing.

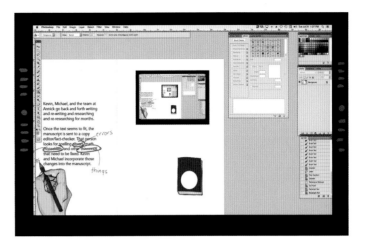

Kevin and Annick will use design software to lay down the images, tweak the colors, and place the text. Just a few years ago, those images and text would have been printed off separately and pasted together on paper, then photographed and reproduced.

We don't even have a physical book yet, and already dozens of people are doing dozens of jobs to get it almost ready for reading.

The wages for all of those people—from editor to art director—now add up to $6,650, or $0.83 per book. Annick plans an initial print run of 8,000 books (so $6,650 divided by 8,000).

At this point, Kevin and Michael also get the second part of their advance, so the TOTAL costs are now up to $16,650 (or $2.08 per book). And we don't even have a physical book yet!

$0.83 + $1.25 = $2.08

WAGES   ADVANCES   COST

Time to get it all down on paper.

Many editors are freelance, which means they aren't employees of the publishing house and are only hired for specific projects. They can live almost anywhere, all over the globe, but they often don't have the same benefits as a full-time employee (things such as health care, pensions, and paid vacations). That can save the publisher money (making the book cheaper). Some freelancers want to work that way. Others don't have a choice—there aren't many full-time editing jobs. Which would you prefer if you had the choice?

Putting It on PAPER

Annick sends the final files to a printer in China.

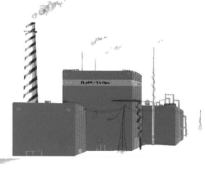

The paper for this book comes from Finland. Trees there are cut down and then shipped to a pulp mill.

Workers turn the logs into chips. Then the chips are sent inside the mill, where they are treated with chemicals, turning them into liquid pulp. That pulp is sent by truck to another plant where it's processed into paper.

The pulp mill pays $30 per ton for the logs. They sell the pulp for about $900 a ton.

The pulp is passed through screens, pressed, and then dried until it binds together in long rolls. For some paper, such as newsprint, this is the final version.

But the paper in this book is glossy and needs to withstand the wear and tear of you flipping through it over and over. So another process, called "finishing," takes place. Chemicals are applied to the paper to make it stronger and help it hold on to the inks better.

The paper is then dried, rolled, and shipped to the printer.

From tree to printing, the paper in this book adds about $0.20 to the printer's costs. The ink adds another $0.50.

Book-printing inks are made from different resins and chemicals. They need to bind tightly with the paper. You don't want to have the pages smudge as you touch them. A factory in New Zealand mixes and adds things such as cyclohexanone (a solvent that evaporates as the ink dries) to shellac, wax, burnt carbon, and other dyes and pigments. Dozens of people work there, from chemists to machinists.

Any chemical process has by-products. Some of these are released into the air. If you've ever smelled a pulp mill, you know what we're talking about. Sulfites, ammonia, and other gases are released as the pulp is made. It can really stink.

The BOOK

The paper is ready. The ink is wet. Time to print!

The text and images are burned onto metal plates. This is done with a precision laser. Even the finest details need to be clear and sharp.

Those plates are then inked, and the paper is fed into large printing presses, which print as many as 1,000 pages a minute.

A production monitor watches the different stages for quality control. He also does test runs to make sure the pages are printing correctly. He might make adjustments to the inks or the plates.

The pages go through a quick drying stage and then get trimmed to the book size.*

There's always a little extra paper left on during the printing process. This gets trimmed and recycled.

A coating of glue binds the assembled pages together along the spine of the book.

The cover is added.

Quality-control workers watch each stage, making sure that the books aren't printing upside down (it happens) or that the pages aren't being cut or folded improperly.

This book is available in both hardcover and paperback. The inside pages are the same, but the hardcover consists of a larger sheet of glossy paper wrapped and glued around a thin piece of pressboard. Endpapers are glued on to cover the seams before the inside pages are glued in place. That's one reason why the hardcover costs more than the paperback.

The printing house has charged Annick $10,000, or $1.25 per book. This covers paper, ink, labor, and a $0.45 per book markup to cover other costs and to ensure a profit.

Annick has now committed $26,650 (or $3.33 for each book) in wages, advances, and production costs.

But there are other costs the publisher now adds to the list.

COSTS for 8,000 books:

Production:	$26,650.00
Marketing:	$6,274.00
Shipping:	$8,366.40
Other (warehouse, rent, insurance, etc.):	$5,400.00
TOTAL:	**$46,690.40**

(or $5.84 per book)

$3.33 + $0.78 + $1.05 + $0.68 = $5.84

PRODUCTION   MARKETING   SHIPPING   OTHER   COST

Now it's time for you to visit the bookstore.

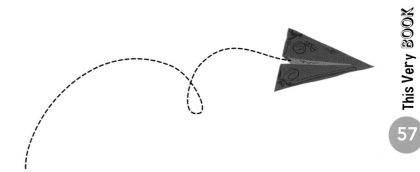

Growing GLOBAL

> Okay, not ready just YET to visit the bookstore.

100 YEARS AGO

Cotton cloth (U.S.A)
Nylon not invented yet!
1,000 km

BACKYARD 0 km

CLOTHES (HANDMADE) 0km

SOAP (LOCAL. MADE FROM ANIMAL FAT) 1 km

leather (CANADA) 300 km

SHOES (ORDERED BY CATALOG. U.S.A.) 1,800 km

TOTAL: 3,101 km (1,926.87 mi)

?

Of course, there's a trade-off here. Products now made in China (for example) have added jobs there. But that also means some jobs have disappeared in North America and Europe. Where are some of your favorite products made? Do you know where they were made 100 years ago?

There's another big part of the global economy we want to look at first. Some products have always traveled a long way to get to market. Tea from China drew traders from England. Spices from India drew Christopher Columbus to look for a way to sail around the globe. Coffee is grown in warm countries and enjoyed everywhere. Chocolate, gasoline, and many other products—and the search for them—have shaped the modern globe.

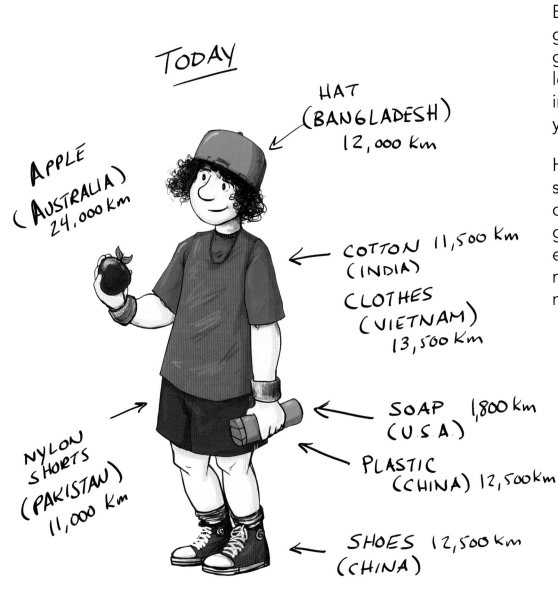

TODAY

HAT
(BANGLADESH)
12,000 km

APPLE
(AUSTRALIA)
24,000 km

COTTON 11,500 km
(INDIA)

CLOTHES
(VIETNAM)
13,500 km

NYLON
SHORTS
(PAKISTAN)
11,000 km

SOAP 1,800 km
(U.S.A.)

PLASTIC
(CHINA) 12,500 km

SHOES 12,500 km
(CHINA)

TOTAL > 98,800 km (61,391.47 mi)

But the size of that global market has grown by gigantic leaps and bounds in just the past 100 years.

Here's where some similar products came from in your great-grandparents' era, and where they might come from now.

Okay, enough time travel. Let's head to the local bookstore.

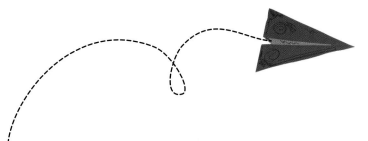

The BOOKSTORE

So far, this book has cost $5.84 to make. So why do you pay $22.95?

Annick sets the retail price of the book—in this case, $22.95. Annick sells the book to the bookstore for $13.77. But that doesn't mean that Annick makes $9.18 in profit. Before the book can get to bookstores, Annick has to pay for distribution and for the commissions of the sales team that sells Annick's books into bookstores in the first place.

The team at Annick is hoping the book will be popular. That means a second printing (or more!) without the editorial costs.

But it can be hard for a book to stand out in the crowd. There are about 350,000 books published each year in North America alone!

Imagine how many people have been involved in making those books!

A mid-sized, independent bookstore has many of the same costs as other stores—wages, insurance, rent, taxes, and so on. That adds up to $7.37 per book. So the bookstore is making a profit of about $1.81 for every copy of this book they sell.

Kevin and Michael will get a royalty of about 10 percent of the "suggested retail price"—or the price you see printed on the book—for every book sold . . . sort of. Remember that they received an "advance on royalties"? That means bookstores will have to sell about 5,000 books before Kevin and Michael start making more money off sales. A bestseller in Canada is about 5,000 books. In the United States and other big markets, it's more like 45,000 books.

COSTS per book:

Wages:	$3.72
Rent and operational costs:	$2.34
Bank services and loans:	$0.44
Utilities:	$0.19
Supplies and services::	$0.23
Other costs:	$0.45
TOTAL:	**$7.37**

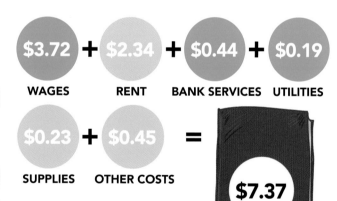

$3.72 + $2.34 + $0.44 + $0.19

WAGES — RENT — BANK SERVICES — UTILITIES

$0.23 + $0.45 =

SUPPLIES — OTHER COSTS

$7.37

COST

So, no one is making a huge profit off one book sale. But lots of people rely on those little bits to add up.

Oh, and a huge thanks to you for choosing this book!

IN CONCLUSION: Between the Covers

So even something as simple as a book is a lot more complicated, and global, than you thought. Authors and illustrators are crucial, but it takes hundreds of people with specific expertise to complete the journey from a good idea to the physical book you are holding in your hands (or reading on your screen).

One final wrinkle. Maybe you bought an electronic book, or e-book. The cost to you was probably $15. But it still cost the publisher all the normal costs to make the book, minus the paper and shipping. Authors usually get 25 percent of the net profits from sales. "Net" refers to the money Annick receives, minus all their costs.

COSTS per book:

Paper:	$0.20
Ink:	$0.50
Wages:	$2.08
Printer (labor and markup):	$0.55
Shipping:	$1.05
Marketing:	$0.78
Sales and Distribution:	$4.68
Other:	$0.68
Annick:	$3.25
Bookstore:	$9.18
TOTAL:	**$22.95**

$0.70 + $5.14 + $4.68 + $3.25 + $7.37 + $1.81 = $22.95

MATERIALS + PRODUCTION + SALES AND DISTRIBUTION + ANNICK + BOOKSTORE COSTS + BOOKSTORE = TOTAL COST

The parts of this book came from all over the world. That's a total of **33,649.92 kilometers (20,909.09 miles)**.

More and more book sales take place online these days. Big sellers such as Amazon.com, Inc. also charge lower prices (usually) than independent or even chain stores. So you can often save money by ordering online. BUT, one big reason e-tailers can do that is that they pay less per book to the publisher. Why? E-tailers are big, and publishers need to be online, so all the power is with the e-tailer. That means the publisher needs to sell a lot more books to make a profit. And that has a ripple effect.

They might begin publishing fewer authors, because they want guaranteed blockbuster sales. That will make it harder for YOU to break in if you want to be an author. And they might have to squeeze their costs—including how much they pay authors, the quality of the paper they use, etc.—in order to make money.

Where do you buy your books?

High TECH

That cell phone in your hand can call anywhere in the world— and it comes from all over the world, too.

We're immersed in technology. Computers, tablets, and, above all, phones are everywhere. There are more than a billion phones sold each year.

Inside are transistors, chips, wires, high-impact glass—and the expertise of thousands of people. This includes the people who make the phone and the people who make sure you can use it.

The journey begins, like with so many products, inside the Earth.

Every phone contains precious metals and minerals. Aluminum, gold, cobalt, platinum, niobium, and tantalum. The last two come from a mineral known as coltan. It's dug, often by hand, in countries such as the Democratic Republic of Congo.

Workers dig pits and then separate the coltan from dirt, rock, and other minerals by sloshing it all in water-filled tubs.

Workers get paid about $0.25 per hour for this work, or $2.50 for a ten-hour workday.

The coltan is crushed into little bits and sent to a processing plant in the United States, where it's refined.

Workers use a lot of energy, and a lot of dangerous chemicals, to strip the bits of coltan apart, separating the niobium and tantalum.

Niobium and tantalum are corrosion resistant, which means they last a long time. They can also carry a lot of electrical charge without overheating—which is crucial for the speed and makeup of modern conductors and chips inside your phone.

There's about $1 worth of niobium and tantalum inside a phone.

The Democratic Republic of Congo has been torn by war for decades. The coltan industry didn't cause that, but sales of coltan have supported weapons purchases on all sides. Some companies have looked for other sources of the mineral. But chances are pretty good that there's coltan from the Democratic Republic of Congo in your devices.

Also, because the industry isn't well regulated, miners have often gone into national parks and forests and animal sanctuaries looking for more deposits of coltan. Does that change how you feel about your tech?

COST

Chips off the OLD BLOCK

The keys to making a phone work? Computer chips, condensers, and processors.

The base for most computer chips, known as a "wafer," is made from silicon.* Silicon is basically sand—one of the most common materials on Earth. It can be melted and formed into incredibly thin chips.

Transistors are etched into the silicon using a process called "photolithography." The metals (including niobium and tantalum) are overlaid on the silicon, along with light-sensitive chemicals, and then the pattern for the circuit layout is photographed onto the chips. There are billions of connections in each chip, and billions of bits of information fire across them every split second, in much the same way that neurons carry information in your brain. Wow!

*Thank those miners again. The silicon in this phone was mined in Brazil.

Technicians in Arizona design new chip patterns. Those patterns are sent to manufacturing plants in China, Ireland, Vietnam, the Netherlands . . . you get the idea.

The chips in this phone were made in Israel.

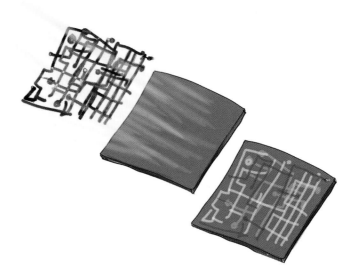

The first computers took up whole buildings but couldn't store as much information as a modern phone.

Jack St. Clair Kilby invented the first chip way back in 1958. To show how well it worked (faster and smaller), he helped design the first pocket calculator. Old calculators were the size of desks!

So far, we've got just the chips—and each one costs about $15. Some are more expensive than others, but the total for all the chips in your phone is about $80.

COSTS per chip:

Silicon:	$0.10
Metals:	$2.00
Manufacturing:	$8.00+
Development:	$5.00+
Spoilage (chips that don't work):	$0.05
TOTAL:	**$15.15+**

$0.10 **+** $2.00 **+** $8.00+ **+** $5.00+ **+** $0.05 **=** $15.15+

SILICON   METALS   MANUFACTURING   DEVELOPMENT   SPOILAGE   COST

Now it's off to the assembly plant! Or is it?

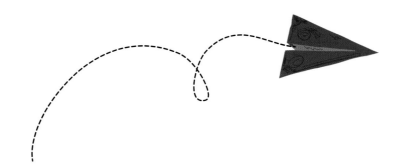

ZAP!

Before we wrap up the cell phone, we need to talk about POWER!

Fracking is a controversial way to get more gas from the Earth. Crews inject a mixture of water, sand, and chemicals into the ground at high pressure. The pressure cracks the rock, releasing the trapped gases. Fracking uses A LOT of water. And numerous studies have linked the practice to earthquakes. If gas was discovered under your home, would you want fracking used to get it out? What if it made your town a lot of money?

Energy—and lots of it—is consumed in every stage of making stuff.

The natural gas for a company in North America is likely from a local source. In Europe, the gas probably comes from Russia—a global power when it comes to power.

Geo-engineers and excavation companies dig down into the Earth and draw out the gas. It's then siphoned off and stored in huge tanks. The tanks can be transported on trains or trucks or pumped through pipelines.

Many countries still burn coal to power their plants. This leads to more air pollution than other sources of energy.

Nuclear power plants provide power by splitting radioactive isotopes, such as uranium. They are cleaner than coal plants when it comes to air pollution, but they also produce waste that needs to be buried deep in the ground. And if something goes wrong, well . . . Boom.

Meltdowns occur when the radioactive material is no longer contained by water or concrete. In 1986, a meltdown in Chernobyl, Ukraine, spewed radioactive material into the air for days. It's still not safe to live close to the blast zone. An earthquake sparked a similar disaster at Japan's Fukushima power plant in 2011.

How much might each kind of energy cost to make a phone?

COSTS of energy:

Natural gas:	$0.10
Nuclear:	$0.04
Hydroelectric:	$0.02
Solar:	$0.22

Hydroelectric dams create lots of power, but they are expensive to build and require flooding vast areas. More than a million people were forced to relocate when China's Three Gorges Dam was constructed.

Solar, wave, and wind power might be the answers of the future, but they aren't straightforward either. The batteries needed to store the energy still require a lot of energy to make, and so far they don't store enough energy to replace cheaper electrical or gas power.

Okay, *now* it's time to put it all together.

Hard Work and HARDWARE

The parts are all manufactured and shipped. Now it's time to assemble them into a phone.

Each of the factories that makes a component in your phone employs hundreds of workers—and that's just for the physical phone. Now Global Phones—and a lot more people—need to add the stuff that makes it work.

Your phone purchase isn't just about performance; it's also about look. And phone companies know that. They employ designers who consider everything from the weight to the feel to the sleek look of your device. That "in your hands" experience can often be the deciding factor in which phone you choose.

Are you willing to pay more for a phone that looks cool, even if a cheaper version works just as well?

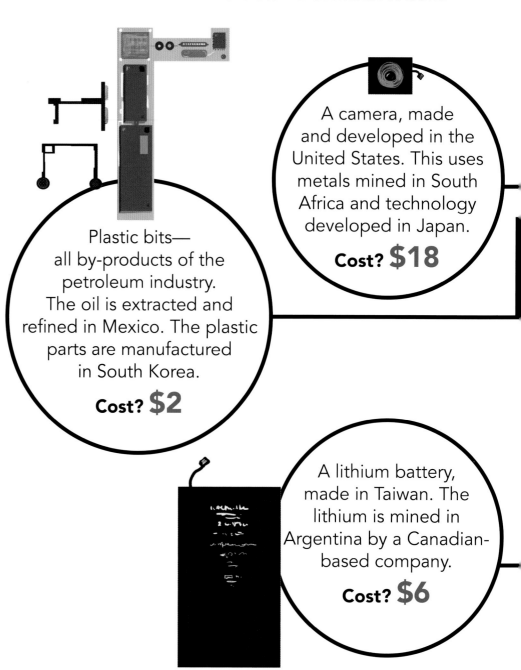

Plastic bits—all by-products of the petroleum industry. The oil is extracted and refined in Mexico. The plastic parts are manufactured in South Korea.

Cost? $2

A camera, made and developed in the United States. This uses metals mined in South Africa and technology developed in Japan.

Cost? $18

A lithium battery, made in Taiwan. The lithium is mined in Argentina by a Canadian-based company.

Cost? $6

Cell phones are made of:

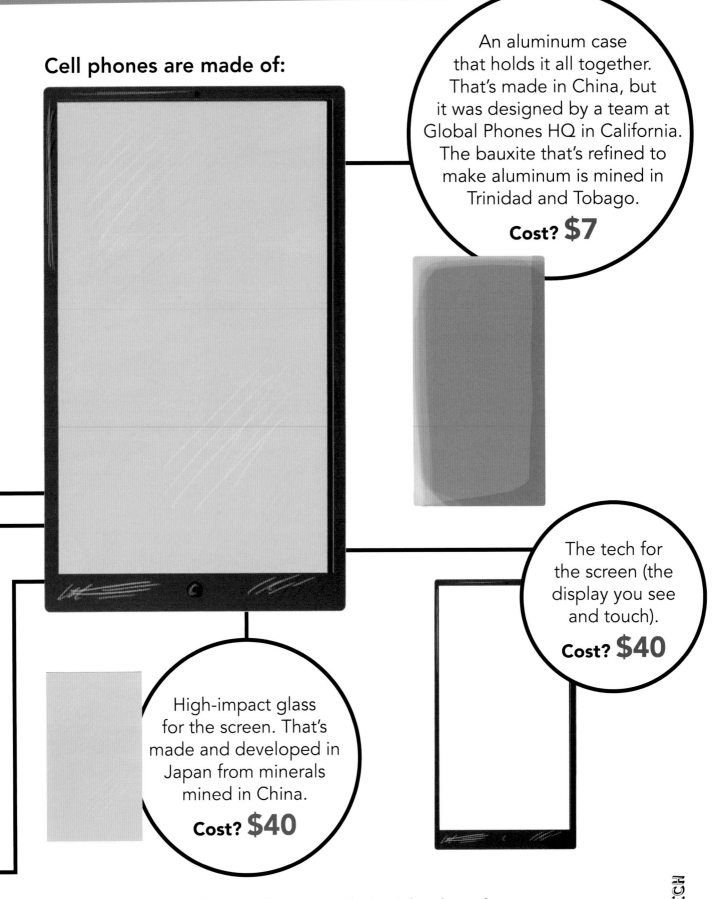

An aluminum case that holds it all together. That's made in China, but it was designed by a team at Global Phones HQ in California. The bauxite that's refined to make aluminum is mined in Trinidad and Tobago.

Cost? $7

The tech for the screen (the display you see and touch).

Cost? $40

High-impact glass for the screen. That's made and developed in Japan from minerals mined in China.

Cost? $40

That's another $113 of materials inside the phone.
Add that to the $80 worth of chips, and you're up to $193.

Hard Work and SOFTWARE

There are two types of software that make your phone work: the operating system and the fun stuff you add later.

The operating system is designed at Global Phones HQ in California. This controls the basics that come with the phone (calling, texting, camera, and so on) and allows new programs to be added later.

Apps (short for "applications") can be designed by big companies or individuals. Let's say you download the Global Giants game (yes, games are apps). It's free, but you can buy more stuff through in-app purchases.

Let's say a phone company spends $1 billion a year researching, developing, and updating its operating systems— or about $20 per phone.

The buildings, the salaries for all the workers (thousands from top to bottom), and so on add another $40 to the price of the phone.

Global Giants was developed by a company in Oslo, Norway, called Glöbalt. Glöbalt designers came up with everything from the graphics to the coding that makes it compatible with your phone's operating system. Glöbalt also has to maintain a server that stores all the player information, game stats, and so on.

Glöbalt spent $150,000 to design the app and spends an additional $100,000 a year to maintain the server. And of course they have to pay lawyers and statisticians and other professionals who make sure the app is patented, protected, and being used.

But if millions of people like the app and either pay money up front or buy the in-app stuff, the company can recoup its investment quickly and make a profit.

We won't add the cost of apps to the final costs for the phone, but it's a cost you will face eventually.

Total costs for the phone itself—so far—are around $253. Time to head to the store.

Companies give a product away for free and then charge more later on. Would you have paid $4.99 for Global Giants? A lot of people would say no. But once you get hooked, you might end up paying way more than that for things like powers, time, or points.

Another trick? You might get a free game, but you have to endure pop-up ads. Would you pay $4.99 to make the ads go away?

Phone SWEET PHONE

> Your phone costs about $250 to make. You buy it for $500. Who gets what?

You might go to the Global Store, which is owned by Global Phones. They sell the phone for $500. You can buy it and decide on a cell service provider later.

Or you might buy the phone at a cell service provider's store. Let's call it Labolg Wireless. They might even "give" you the phone for free when you sign up for their plan (kind of like those game apps). But, really, the cost of the phone is added into whatever you pay Labolg each month. So, you pay the same amount as you would at the Global Store; it's just spread over the term of your contract.

There are costs to run a store, whether it's owned by Global or Labolg. Let's say that wages, rent, insurance, electricity, and all the other costs add another $10 to the cost of the phone.

COSTS per phone:

Manufacturing and raw materials:	$250.00
Store:	$10.00
Markup:	$240.00
TOTAL:	**$500.00**

$250 + **$10** + **$240** = **$500**

MANUFAC-
TURING
AND RAW
MATERIALS

STORE

MARKUP

COST

Yes, phone companies make a lot of profit from phone sales—and that money goes to many different places.

Some goes to pay the shareholders who have invested in the company.

Some goes to pay for expansion—more factories, more jobs.

Some goes to pay for research and development—designing the next generation of phones, operating systems, and hardware.

And some covers losses from Global Phones' less successful products—like the tablets that didn't sell so well last year.

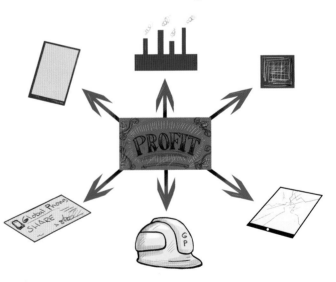

But the costs to you aren't done yet. There are hundreds of thousands of people helping you make each call, send each text, and check out where you need to go.

Making the CALL

A phone is just a pretty paperweight until you get onto a network.

Let's say you want to send a text to a friend on the other side of the world. How does that work, and who makes it happen?

Relay towers broadcast cell phone calls, texts, and searches. As you move around during the day, your phone switches from one tower to the next, automatically searching out the closest. The information you send (a text in this case) gets encoded and sent at super-high speed from tower to tower until it reaches your friend.

Along the way, it might even get a boost from a satellite along the way to speed things up.

Satellite phones send signals into space and back to Earth directly. Not all phones have satellite antennas, but cell service providers still use satellites to send information from a tower in, say, China to a phone in Argentina.

So, you've got a lot of experts and workers involved here.

Scientists study microwaves (the actual waves, not the ovens!) and how they travel over distances.

Engineers figure out how to build the hardware to make network relays work.

Governments were the first players in the satellite industry, largely for military reasons. The Americans and the Soviets raced to control space. The U.S.S.R. sent up Sputnik 1 in 1957. The U.S. sent up SCORE (Signal Communications by Orbital Relay Equipment) in December 1958. These days, private companies do most of the launches.

Construction workers assemble and maintain the towers you see in fields or on the tops of buildings.

Rocket scientists and engineers figure out ways to shoot satellites out of the atmosphere.

There are solar panels that power a satellite during its lifetime orbiting Earth, so the people who develop those are helping out as well.

All of these costs are spread out over all the subscribers to a network provider.

Let's say you pay Labolg Wireless $100 a month. How does that break down?

COSTS:

Access fee for basics:	$40
Data (60 GB):	$60
TOTAL:	**$100**

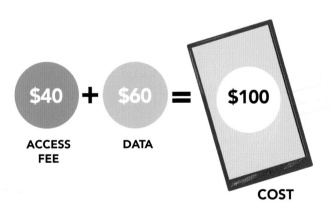

$40 + $60 = $100

ACCESS FEE   DATA   COST

The company is really only spending about $40 to provide you those services. The rest goes to pay for other costs (wages, infrastructure, etc.).

IN CONCLUSION:
Adding It Up on Your Calculator App!

So let's see what all the technology has cost from rock to rocket to pocket.

The phone in your hand started as a rock in the ground, or sand on the beach.

And the people who transformed it (and keep it working) are from all over the globe.

If we imagine the chain of production as a cell signal—well, it's been pretty much everywhere on the globe.

COSTS per phone:

Raw materials:	$16.00
Energy:	$0.38
Wages:	$20.62
Manufacturing:	$40.00
Hardware:	$113.00
Software:	$60.00
Store costs:	$10.00
Markup:	$240.00
TOTAL:	**$500.00**

$80.00 CHIPS + $113.00 HARDWARE + $60.00 SOFTWARE + $7.00 WAGES AND DEVELOPMENT + $240.00 MARKUP = $500.00 TOTAL COST

The total distance (not including the signals that bounce off satellites) is **45,336.15 kilometers (28,170.58 miles)**.

Cell phones have become a huge part of our lives. They've made it easier to talk and text and connect with friends and to find information. But there are trade-offs. New injuries such as "texting thumb" are cropping up, along with neck and back pain. Some people can become addicted to the constant sense of connection. And there may be links between cell-phone addiction and increased anxiety and poor sleep. How much time do you spend on your phone?

See the BIG PICTURE?

> More than half the people in the world need some help seeing. BUT... we're going to let you in on a little secret right off the top.

Here it goes . . .

We had a *really* hard time determining exactly how much it costs to make a pair of eyeglasses.

And we are good at this. We have given accurate (if estimated) costs throughout this book and in *Follow Your Money*, but this chapter really stumped us.

We can tell you that if you have a strong prescription, you might pay about $400 for a pair of glasses. The frames might cost you $150, and you might be charged $250 for the lenses.

We can even tell you that in those glasses, to the best of our knowledge, the raw materials only cost about $25—$16 for plastic and about $9 for other materials, including metals.

Plastics, even really high-grade ones, are not that expensive to make or buy. Even metal frames contain only a few cents' worth of materials.

The metals are mined in various places, including Brazil, China, the United States, and Australia.

A lab technician cuts your lens from a "lens blank"—usually a thick piece of plastic (from the petroleum industry) or sometimes glass (from minerals mined in China and processed in Japan). This can be quite thick—10.1 by 3.8 centimeters (4 by 1.5 inches).

And, yes, there is always research and development going on to make harder plastics, more scratchproof surfaces, etc. And, yes, just like all the other products in this book, there are lots of people involved, from designers and opticians to chemists and miners.

We'll estimate that all of this adds, total, another $50 to the cost of your glasses. But we can't say for sure.

Why? Keep reading . . .

The Picture Is SMUDGY

One reason is that a single company, Luxottica, makes and sells almost all the frames you can buy, no matter what name is actually on the frame. They also own and run many of the stores and are getting more involved in making lenses.

This means they control the "chain of production"—from raw materials to you buying the product.

This lack of competition means Luxottica can set the prices they want, and their markups can be huge—more than 50 percent. So they might sell the lenses to a store (even if they own it) for $30 and the frames for $100 and then sell them for $60 and $200.

But, again, that's an estimate. Luxottica is a private company, so they don't have to release information on how their company works or what it actually costs them to make their product. So we can't say for sure what they spend on the other parts of the process.

You can read the company's financial statements on their website, but while they list the company's costs, expenses, and profits, they don't say how much it actually costs to make the products. And this raises a couple of really interesting questions about the global economy.

The science behind glasses has been around for thousands of years. Although the Ancient Egyptians wrote about the abilities of curved glass to bend light, the first actual eyeglasses were probably invented around 1200. Italian monks were able to grind quartz into concave shapes. They held it over text and, voilà, larger words! Those concave shapes were essentially handheld magnifying glasses. Spectacles began to appear in paintings about 100 years later.

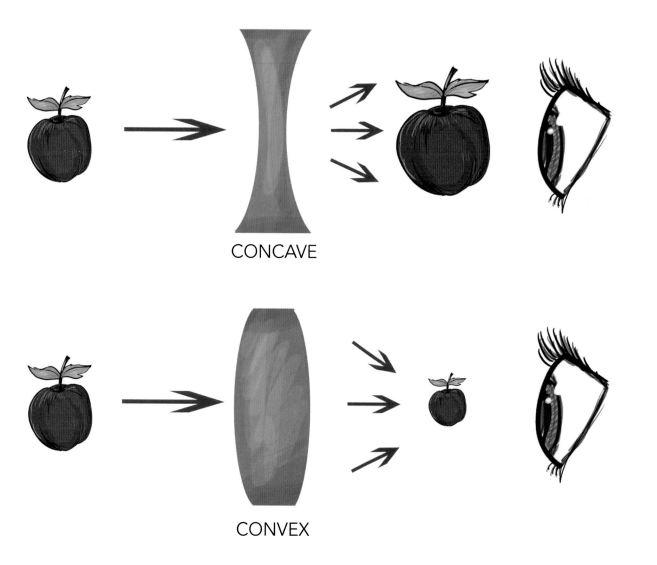

CONCAVE

CONVEX

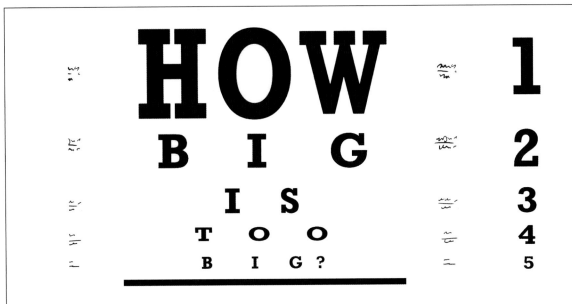

HOW BIG IS TOO BIG?

QUESTION ONE: How big is too big?

Globalization can make it easier to grab a whole market. For example, it's now easier to reach millions of people (or "consumers") quickly. This is the growing "scale" of the global economy.

A $1 profit per sale wasn't much when you could only sell 10,000 of something to a local market. But if you can sell 100 million of something (because the global economy is HUGE), you can make a LOT of money. And companies use that profit to buy up and absorb smaller companies. So the companies get bigger and more global, too.

Huge companies can skew the balance of the market. If companies can charge whatever they want and control the market completely, consumers don't have any choice but to pay that price.

So governments have traditionally worked to break up companies that get too big or that control the market for one product. They refer to these giants as "monopolies"—companies that can tilt the market in their favor because of their size.

And where there's money, there's greed. Everyone would like to make a profit, but for some people there's no limit to that desire. Which leads to . . .

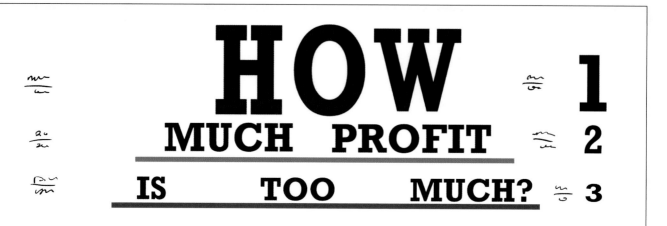

HOW MUCH PROFIT
IS TOO MUCH?

 QUESTION TWO: How much profit is too much?

You might get angry reading this book and finding out that companies can charge you way more for a product than it costs to make it. But profit is a complex topic. The amount the company makes goes to pay shareholders and to pay back banks that have lent them money. We've talked about this throughout the book (and could write a whole other book just about this). Employees also need to get paid.

How much would you charge if you sold, say, a pair of shoes or a video game you made? Do you think people would pay more or less than that?

And if people are willing to pay the price, is it too high? People who want a "free market" (meaning free from government controls) argue that rising prices will send consumers looking for cheaper products elsewhere. That is happening (a little) with online sales.

But, again, the global market can make this easier and harder. Yes, you can now buy products from anywhere in the world and have them delivered to your door, which can make it easier to search for cheaper alternatives.

But there's a good chance the product you buy is made by the same company that sells through your local store. And if they are global and control the market, they can set any price they want.

Not everyone owns stock (shares in a company). In fact, studies show that almost all stock is owned by just a few wealthy people (about 10 percent of the world population). BUT if you use a bank, you are indirectly involved. Banks lend money to companies and also invest in stock.

IN CONCLUSION? Maybe?

So, what can we confidently say? Not much. But these are our best guesses.

Your pair of glasses starts with a visit to an optometrist. She has you look at specialized charts (made in Washington state) and examines your eyes using an aberrometer (made in California) and various other instruments. Once she determines what lenses you need, she sends that information to a laboratory where your lenses will be made to order.

The optometrist visit might cost you $100, depending on how many tests she runs. Or it might be "free" if your exam takes place at the eyeglass store. (They'll still fold the cost of the optometrist into the costs of running the store.)

The coolest-looking machine in the optometrist's office is the phoropter (made in Buffalo, New York)—the device with all the dials. It allows the optometrist to fine-tune the prescription for your eyes.

We said you might pay $400 for the glasses. How does that break down? Here's our best shot.

COSTS per pair of eyeglasses:

Lenses:	$30.00
Frames:	$100.00
Extras (anti-glare or scratch-resistant coatings, etc.):	$25.00
Store (machinery, materials):	$127.50
TOTAL:	**$282.50**
PROFIT (about a 30% margin):	**$117.50**

$30 LENSES + $100 FRAMES + $25 EXTRAS + $127.50 STORE = $282.50 TOTAL COST

We can say that the stuff in the glasses (and the people who got it where it needed to be) span the globe—covering 38,538.95 kilometers (23,947.00 miles).

Frames bought online can be cheaper, because the e-tailer doesn't have to cover the costs of running a physical store. But you still have to handle the rest of the transaction—from getting your prescription to making sure the frames fit. And the frames might still be made by Luxottica, or they could be made by a smaller company, likely in China. Would you trade the "in-person" experience for online sales?

The Concluding CONCLUSION

PART ONE

The global economy is complex and gigantic.

We cannot stress enough that this book is only a useful introduction to the complex questions (economic, ethical, and personal) that are involved in each and every transaction.

But we want you, above all, to realize that a human being stands at each link in that "chain."

Every small item you own, buy, or use depends on the hard work and expertise of thousands of people around the globe.

The miner in the Democratic Republic of Congo might not be aware that the coltan she is mining will help make your phone. The farmer in China doesn't necessarily know that the cotton she grows will end up as the shirt on your back.

But if those people don't do their jobs, and do them well, the chain breaks. So the next time you zip up your backpack, thank the miner in Brazil who helped extract the iron ore to make steel. Then thank the workers at the steel plant in Canada and the people at the zipper-manufacturing plant in New Jersey. And don't forget the sewers and cutters at the textile shop in Bangladesh who assembled the backpack.

Oh, and then thank the drivers and sailors who shipped the raw materials from point to point, and the workers who packaged the finished product so it wouldn't get wrecked on its way to the store.

And don't forget to thank the store owners and employees who helped you find what you want.

And don't just thank them . . . pay them.

The price of everything you buy is split up into smaller and smaller bits between more and more people. That cutter at the textile factory in Guatemala might need the few pennies she gets to feed her family. She might need more, and maybe that "more" is something you should be willing to pay for the shirt on your back.

The Concluding CONCLUSION

PART TWO

You are part of this system.

It's part of your responsibility as a consumer to think about your role in the economy.

Yes, the phone company that sells you a $500 cell phone might make a lot of profit. But the people who make the silicon chips only get a few dollars. And the further you get from the finished product, the smaller the bits—and the more precious they are to the people who get them.

So while we're talking about responsibility, here's a solid piece of advice:

Don't steal art. The musician might be famous and rich, but the studio engineer who helped mix the final songs needs the $0.50 she gets from every sale. An author might be rich and famous (ha!), but the bookstore owner needs the money he makes off the markup to pay for salaries, heat, rent, and food.

Remember, this is the same system you'll enter when you become a worker. How will you want to be treated? How will you want to be paid?

You might think the job you do isn't as "important" as someone else's. But every job is important, and every job creates ripples that can reach around the globe.

If a dishwasher doesn't wash the dishes well in a restaurant, it doesn't matter how great the chef is because someone is going to get sick.

The cleaners at a computer-chip laboratory better make sure there's no dust or dirt around, because even a speck can ruin thousands of dollars' worth of high tech.

If the paper in this book isn't up to standard, the ink will smudge all over your fingers, or the book will fall apart after you read it once.

This book barely touches on the complexity of our global economy. But we hope this glimpse makes you appreciate just how connected we all are here on planet Earth.

References and
FURTHER READING

Educators:
Check out annickpress.com/Follow-Your-Stuff
for a free lesson plan and our series of online video casts
you can use in your classrooms on some of our book's trickier
concepts such as relative value, greed,
and more.

Here are some great resources for looking at the global economy and maybe for finding your own answers to some of the questions you encountered in this book.

1 Toasted!

Near the beginning of the book, we talked about how complicated it really is to make something "from scratch." Thomas Thwaites proved it. One day, he wondered why he was paying $15 or so for a plastic toaster. How hard would it be to make one himself? Well, $2,000 or so later, he had . . . well, not really a toaster. You can watch a very funny TED Talks video he made here: ted.com/talks/thomas_thwaites_how_i_built_a_toaster_from_scratch

2 Fair Wages?

Throughout the book, we looked at the disparity between wages in countries such as the United States and Canada and countries such as India, China, or Guatemala.The U.S. Department of Labor tracks wages across all sorts of industries (bls.gov). The International Labour Organization does the same thing around the globe (ilo.org).

3 Smell Alert!

A pulp mill made the paper you're holding right now. We talked a bit about how much a mill can smell, and that's one of the trade-offs the economy asks us to consider (smell vs. need). Here's a good explanation of how and why the smells happen: dhs.wisconsin.gov/air/pulpodors.htm

4 A Chip off the Old Sand Dune

Intel is one of the biggest computer-chip manufacturers in the world. You can search for their website. They also have this video showing the process from sand to chip: youtube.com/watch?v=Q5paWn7bFg4

5 See for Yourself
Luxottica is a global superpower when it comes to eyeglasses. We admit we had a very hard time working out how much the glasses cost to make. The company does post annual reports. You can read them for yourself: luxottica.com/en/investors/annual-reports-and-publications

6 Researching Commodities

We talked about commodities in the chapter on T-shirts. Commodity prices can dip or rise dramatically based on supply, demand, wars . . . lots of different reasons.

Try keeping track of how the price of cotton (or coffee, or rice, or almost anything) changes over time. You can do that here (the site updates prices every day): indexmundi.com/commodities

Then see if you can find a connection between something that happened in the news and a dip or spike in the price.

7 Human Rights

We mentioned human rights (and abuses of them) numerous times. There are many organizations that monitor how workers are treated in the global economy.

United Nations: un.org
Human Rights Watch: hrw.org
KAIROS: kairoscanada.org

There are plenty more, so do some searching on your own!

8 What Fits in a Box?

We came across a fun page from a company in China. They ask their customers to figure out how many products they can fit into a shipping container.

theodmgroup.com/how-many-products-fit-in-a-container

9 Take a Deep Breath . . .

We touched on the complicated reasons that a puffer might cost a lot in one country and less in another. *The New York Times* took a look at this same issue a few years back: nytimes.com/2013/10/13/us/the-soaring-cost-of-a-simple-breath.htm

10 Taking Stock

Another story that is worth a LOT more digging is the question of stock ownership. Yes, companies have to pay shareholders portions of their profits, and that's fair since shareholders take risks lending money to companies.

BUT the system has become very top-heavy, with fewer and fewer people (the wealthy) actually able to buy and own stock. *TIME* magazine had a quick look at the situation:

time.com/money/5054009/stock-ownership-10-percent-richest

INDEX

ABOUT THE AUTHORS

Kevin Sylvester wishes he understood the economy better. (You probably wish you did too.) That's why Kevin hangs around with smart people such as Michael Hlinka . . . to try to figure out complicated stuff. What Kevin does have is curiosity. He wants to know as much as he can about how everything works—sports, space travel, cooking, bikes, cars, and money. And he loves to draw.

This has led him down many interesting roads and has led to many books. *Follow Your Stuff* is only his latest book with Annick. There was, of course, *Follow Your Money*, but also *Basketballogy*, *Baseballogy*, *GameDay*, and *Showtime*. He writes novels too!

He has a book called *Mucus Mayhem* about a girl who can make her boogers come to life. His sci-fi trilogy MINRs is a bestseller and critical success.

His cooking mystery collection, Neil Flambé Capers, is now at six books. And picture books! *Super-Duper Monster Viewer*, *Splinters* and his brand-new *Gargantua (Jr.) Defender of Earth*!

Kevin also does more than a hundred school presentations per year —featuring farting contests, five-second cartooning classes, and cat poop coffee.

Michael Hlinka wishes he was more creative. (You might wish you were too.) That's why Michael hangs out with imaginative people such as Kevin Sylvester.

What Michael does have is high energy and a strong work ethic.

During the day he teaches business courses at George Brown College, and during evenings and on the weekend he runs two different programs for the University of Toronto School of Continuing Studies.

In his spare time, Michael likes to work out and play all the sports in the world with his wife and son.